Must-Know Vocab

Decoden: a highly stylized, colorful, and over-the-top Japanese decorative craft that literally means "phone decoration," but which has grown to encompass all sorts of fun projects. It involves decorating objects with lots of charms and bling.

Collage clay: also known as frosting or whippy, a useful material that is perfect for decoden. You can embed charms, stones, and the like in the clay and it will harden for a permanent finish.

Cabochon: a catchall word for all sorts of little charms, trinkets, and findings that you can use to make decoden.

16

Rainbow Cell Phone Case

18

Breakfast Special Jar

20

Chocoholic Trinket Box

22

No Time Like the
Present Frame

24

Silver Sparkle Jewelry Set

26

Deco Nails

28

Upcycled Headband

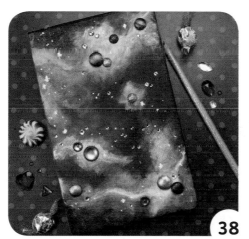

Decoden Supplies

Ready to deco? Here are some basic tools and supplies you need to get started adorning your favorite items. What you need depends on how far and how customized you want to go!

Cabochons and Findings

They can be called a number of things: trinkets, charms, cabs, and the like, but they all mean little bits and baubles that can be glued to your projects for decoden. They come in all kinds of shapes and sizes, from fake food to cute animals, and can be made from plastic, metal, glass, or resin. You can buy them online, find them in the jewelry or scrapbooking section of your craft store, or even take apart a clearance necklace to get some truly interesting pieces. (If shopping online, keyword searches for cabochon, kawaii, and charm will net you lots of results.) Or you can go completely custom and make your own!

Making your own charms

Polymer clay: To make really unique charms, you can sculpt your own from polymer clay. Fimo and Sculpey are two reliable brands that come in amazing colors so you don't have to paint the finished charm. A quick dip in glaze or polyurethane also gives your charm a bright shine. See the techniques starting on page 8 for some sculpting tips, or you can always use silicone molds to easily form charms.

Mod Melts: For a much quicker collection than clay sculpting, Plaid has developed a faux-resin material called Mod Melts. The sticks work like hot glue sticks that you use to fill their collection of silicone molds, and they come in metallic, colored, glitter, and translucent varieties. The result is a finished cabochon that feels just like resin and can easily be painted, decorated, and adhered to your projects. See how to use them on page 8.

Tiny Trinkets: Rhinestones, Pearls, and Studs

Rhinestones: These are used for either the blinged-out look or to add some extra sparkle to your composition. High-end rhinestones are typically made from glass, while more affordable ones are made from acrylic. Make sure to get flat-back rhinestones if you're planning to decorate a flat surface, as they will lay nice and even on your project.

Pearls: Another welcome addition to both cute and glamorous decoden is the use of pearls; they come in lots of colors and sizes, so they go along perfectly with rhinestone compositions. Flat-back pearls can be found for gluing directly onto your project, while round pearl beads settle nicely into collage clay.

Studs: Metal studs are often the kind you see on leather clothing, but they can be added to decoden as well. Flat-back metal studs are ideal, but studs with prongs on the back can be used as well, as long as the prongs are bent back with jewelry pliers. You can find them in many geometric shapes, sizes, and metal colors; studs can be glued on nicely with jewelry adhesive or tucked into collage clay.

Handle with care

Rhinestones get their distinctive sparkle from the reflective foil backing behind each stone. Rough handling or moving the stone after it has been glued can cause this backing to peel off (especially with less expensive rhinestones). Once this happens, the stone will look dull, like regular glass or plastic, so be delicate with your stones to avoid this.

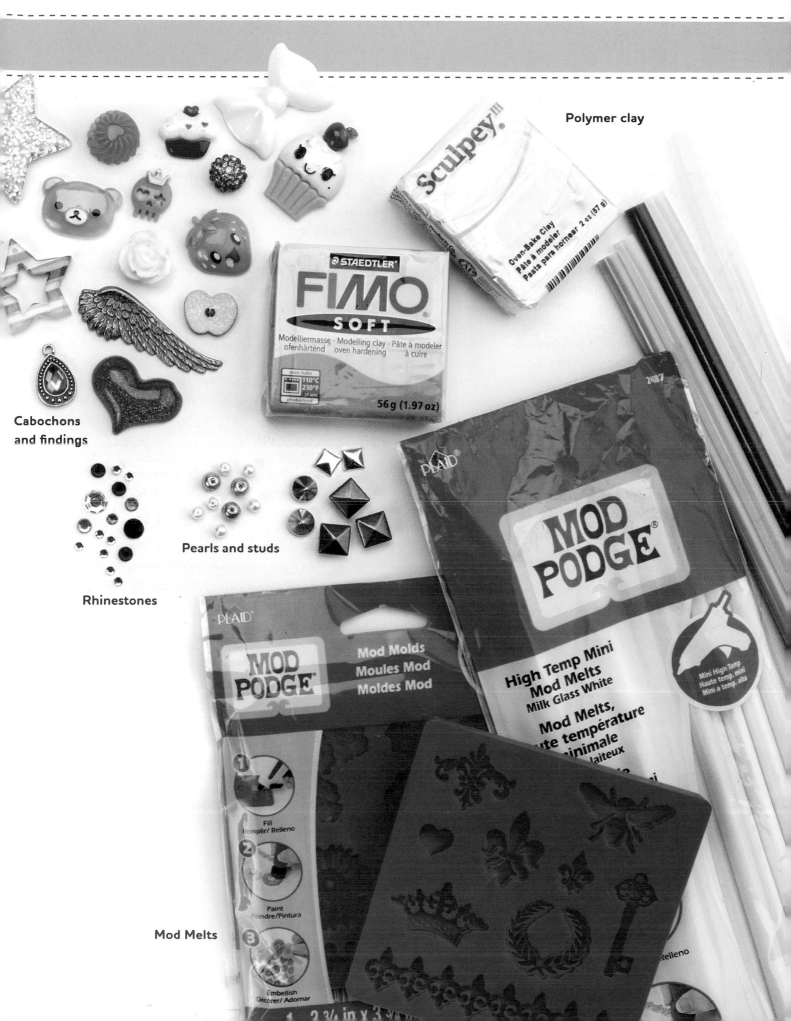

Polymer clay

Cabochons
and findings

Pearls and studs

Rhinestones

Mod Melts

Adhesives

Collage clay/silicone: Known in the decoden world as "whippy" or "frosting," this is the fluffy stuff used to adhere your charms and trinkets to your project in a bed of whipped icing. Decoden crafters outside of Japan typically resort to 100% silicone caulk (a bathroom sealant) found in hardware stores, but Plaid has recently released a product called Collage Clay that's nontoxic and made specifically for decoden frosting. It comes in vanilla and strawberry (colors, not flavors!) in ready-to-pipe bags complete with piping tips. Because it is a bit messy, a non-stick work mat is a real plus.

Glue: If the fluffy frosting isn't quite your style, you can adhere your trinkets and rhinestones with glue instead. There are a few trusted glues to choose from that each behave differently; you may want to try all of them over time to see which you like best.

- **E-6000 glue** is a well-known glue that is very thick and viscous. You can apply your items once the glue becomes tacky, and they stick quite easily.
- **GS Hypo Cement glue** has a slightly thinner consistency for easy spreading and comes in a needle-nose tube that is very easy to control for precise application.
- **Hobby epoxy** (such as Quik-Cure 5 Min. Epoxy by Hobbylinc) is found in hobby shops more often than craft shops and is often used for assembling models. This glue has two parts that must be mixed and then applied to your surface.

Tools

Pick-up tool/pencil: When handling tiny trinkets, you'll want a very precise tool to set the pieces just where you want them. You'll want either plastic tools or pencils where one end is a slightly sticky substance (such as wax). This will stick to your rhinestones just enough to pick them up so you can place them without leaving a residue. You can also try making your own tool like this by dipping a pointed object (such as a chopstick or thin knitting needle) into melted wax until you get a little ball on one end.

Tweezers: Tweezers are ideal for any other time you want to move your stones or if pickup tools feel clunky to you. A pair from around the house usually works, but you can also find beading tweezers made specifically for handling rhinestones and beads along with the other jewelry tools at your local craft store.

Finishing Touches

Acrylic paint: Easy and inexpensive to use on both Mod Melt cabochons and polymer clay trinkets, acrylic paint comes in lots of different colors and finishes, so no two charms are exactly alike! See the techniques on page 12 for some tricks to use with acrylic paint.

Puffy/drizzle paints: This thick paint is easy to draw with and dries while maintaining its puffy 3-D shape. It's perfect for creating "icing" drizzles on sweet decoden projects.

Beads: While large beads work nicely as cabochons, tiny beads such as seed beads, crystal beads, or bugle beads add nice filler to cute decoden projects. Seed and bugle beads even look like sprinkles!

Glitter: For that last bit of sparkle, glitter is the ultimate coup de grace. A tiny sprinkling on wet collage clay, glue, or clay glaze is enough to make it stick. I used the Mod Podge® Podgeable Glitters from Plaid to get just the right amount of glitter with no mess.

Adhesives

Beads

Paints

Tweezers

Pick-up tool

Glitter

Using Mod Melts

Instead of buying cabochons and charms, Mod Melts are an easy way of making your own. The Mod Melt stick works just like a glue stick with your favorite glue gun and the accompanying silicone molds. Here's how to make them and get well on your way to building a huge collection of cabochons!

1. Fill the mold. After inserting your Mod Melt stick into your glue gun and allowing it to heat up, fill the mold of your choice by squeezing the trigger as you normally would. Start down in the crevices of the mold and work your way up to be sure each tiny cranny is filled.

2. Pop out the charm. Allow the charm to cool for about 10 minutes until it has completely hardened. Then pop it out by bending back the mold.

3. Trim the charm. If you have an extra ridge on the side of your finished charm, it can be trimmed away with a pair of tiny scissors or a crafting knife.

Sculpting with Polymer Clay

If you can't find quite the right mold for the charms you imagined, you can try making your own from polymer clay! Not only is it easy to use because you bake it at home, but it comes in loads of colors. Here are some simple instructions for building a collection of fake sweets.

Cookie/Biscuit

We all love a good chocolate chip cookie, but traditional shortbread biscuits are so much cuter and ripe for decorating!

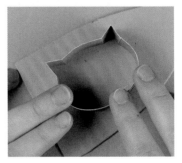

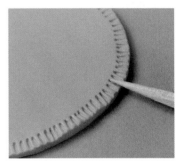

1. Cut the shape. Using a cookie cutter or cutting freehand, cut the shape you want from a sheet of rolled clay, about ⅛" (0.3cm) thick.

2. Add a ridged texture. Using a toothpick or similar tool, press ridges around the perimeter of the cookie that are perpendicular to the edge of the shape.

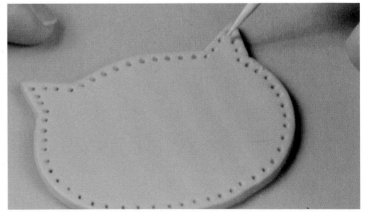

3. Add a dotted texture. Alternatively, you can use dots for a different look. Using a toothpick or similar tool, poke dots around the perimeter of the cookie. When finished, consider brushing the cookie with pastel chalk powder (technique on page 12) for a fresh-baked look!

Macarons

These delicious French cookie sandwiches are usually made from almond flour, egg whites, and sweet fillings, but here's how to make them from clay in every flavor!

1. Create the top. Start with two chunks of clay about the same size and big enough to fit into a round measuring spoon (a half-teaspoon is used here). Press one of the clay pieces into the measuring spoon and squish it inside so one side is flat and leaves a prominent ridge around the shape. If you find your clay sticks to the spoon, try dusting it with cornstarch beforehand.

2. Flatten the top. Using a flat object, press down on the top of the dome to create a flat top on your cookie. Make sure not to flatten it so much that the ridge at the bottom is no longer prominent.

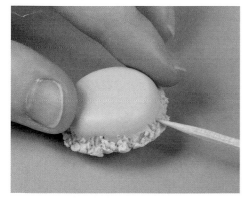

3. Texture the ridge. Using a toothpick or a needle, poke the ridge surrounding the cookie until it's textured nicely, going in swirls and zigzags with the point until you get a nice foamy look. This is the "foot" of your cookie, which occurs in the baking process of the actual food.

4. Create the sandwich. Repeat steps 1–3 with the other chunk of clay for the second half of your cookie. Bake both halves of the cookie and, when cool, sandwich them together with a dollop of collage clay. At this point you can tuck some rhinestones or beads into the filling or wait until the filling is dry and glue a charm to the top.

Foolproof Baking

If you've ever had a problem with your polymer clay burning in the oven, try out this low-and-slow method that works every time. Best of all, it works for all thicknesses of clay, so you can cook your charms all at once regardless of size.

1. Place your clay piece on a cookie sheet lined with aluminum foil or parchment paper and place in a cold oven.

2. Heat the oven to 200°F (93°C). Set a timer for 20 minutes.

3. When the timer finishes, increase the temperature to 225°F (107°C). Set a timer for 20 minutes.

4. When the timer finishes, increase the temperature to 250°F (121°C). Set a timer for 20 minutes.

5. When the timer finishes, turn the oven off. Crack the oven door and allow the clay to cool for 20 minutes.

6. Once the clay is cool, remove the clay from the oven and allow it to come to room temperature before painting or adding to your project.

Pretzel Rods/Cookie Sticks

Chocolate and candy coated pretzel rods and cookie sticks are just perfect for extra embellishment. They have lots of surface area for sprinkles, icing drizzles, and glitter, and they look adorable, too!

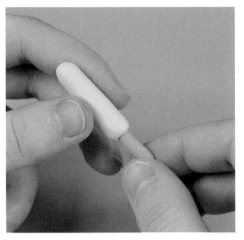
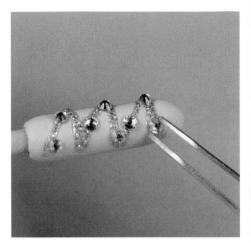

1. Create the stick. Roll a snake of brown or tan clay that's about ¼" (0.5cm) in diameter. Cut a 2" (5cm)-long section and bake it halfway by following only steps 1–2 of the Foolproof Baking technique, page 9.

2. Add the coating. Roll a thin layer of clay for your candy coating, about ⅛" (0.3cm) thick. Cut a small section about 1" x 1" (2.5 x 2.5cm) and wrap it around the end of your stick. Seal the seam in the back by pushing the clay together.

3. Finish the stick. Bake the finished cookie stick completely (following all the steps of the Foolproof Baking technique, page 9), then add icing drizzles, sprinkles, and other bits as you like!

Sprinkles

This adds the finishing touch to any fake dessert!

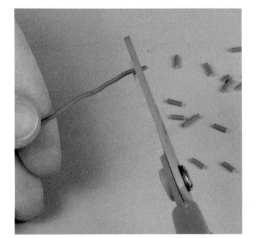
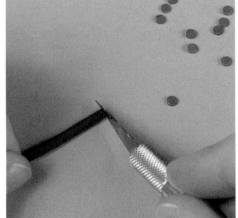
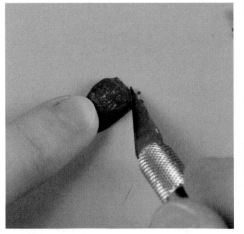

Long sprinkles. Roll or use a clay extruder to make a very thin snake. Bake the snake halfway (following steps 1–2 of the Foolproof Baking technique, page 9), and then cut small lengths from it. Finish baking the small bits as before.

Round sprinkles. Roll or use a clay extruder to make a thin snake, about ⅛" (0.3cm) wide. Bake the snake halfway (following steps 1–2 of the Foolproof Baking technique, page 9), and then slice small discs from it. Finish baking the small bits as before.

Chunks. Shape a large oval about ½" (1.5cm) thick out of clay and cut random chunks from it. Bake the chunks halfway (following steps 1–2 of the Foolproof Baking technique, page 9), and then cut smaller bits from the larger chunks. Finish baking the small bits as before.

Ice Cream Scoops

Create a scoop of ice cream that looks almost good enough to eat! Using just a few techniques, you can make a sundae in all your favorite flavors.

1. Gather your clay colors. Gather three colors of clay: a large ball of your main color, another about half as large of a complementing color, and the last about one-eighth as large of a contrasting color.

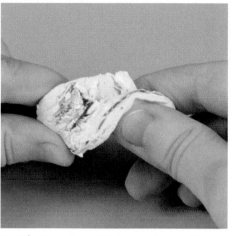

2. Mix the clay. Mix the colors with your hands with a swirling motion until you're happy with the mixture. When you like the swirls, roll the mixed clay into a sphere.

3. Create the base. Press the mixed ball of clay into a round measuring spoon and press it flat so a ridge extends around the bottom. If you find your clay sticks to the spoon, try dusting it with cornstarch beforehand.

4. Texture the top. Texture the ridge of the scoop with a toothpick as in step 3 of the macaron tutorial (page 9). Crinkle up a small ball of aluminum foil and run it over the top of your ice cream scoop to give it an interesting texture. A used toothbrush works nicely as well.

Tools at Hand

You can accomplish a lot with just your hands and a bit of polymer clay, but you might find it easier to use some tools for more delicate work. While they do make specialized clay tools for smoothing, texturing, rolling, and the like, you can also achieve a lot of these same effects by using what you have around the house. Plastic silverware works for cutting, measuring spoons are great for dome molds, and toothpicks and wooden craft sticks are perfect texturing tools.

Painting Tips

There's much more you can do with paint than you might think. Check out these tips to give your charms an interesting paint job, or even learn how to tint your collage clay different colors!

Painting Small Items

Because cabochons can be so small, it's hard to get an even coating of paint without making a mess of yourself. Consider using adhesive putty (also called mounting adhesive, sticky tack, etc.), to hold the charm in place onto a protected workspace (like newspaper on a table) while you paint it from all sides.

Dry Brushing

Add another dimension to your paint job by dabbing contrasting paint over your first coat with a dry brush. Make sure your first coat has fully dried; the second layer of paint will just cover the prominent areas, making a nice contrast. This technique is also used on the Industrial Chic cell phone case on page 17.

Coloring Collage Clay

You can make your own colors of collage clay and silicone by adding a few drops of saturated acrylic paint.

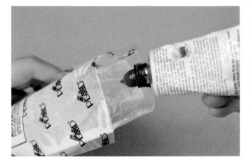

1. Add the paint. When your bag of collage clay is about a third to halfway empty (giving you more room to mix), cut it open by slitting the very top edge. Add just a dollop or two of dark paint to create a nice tint.

Before You Bake

Here's a trick for painting your clay *before* you bake it with pastel chalk powder. Using a simple set of pastel chalks, you can create some amazing, soft effects, and you'll know your hard work is baked right in!

1. Scrape the chalk. Using a craft knife, carefully scrape the side of your chalk pastel to create a fine powder on your work surface. This way, you can mix colors until you get a combination you like.

2. Dust the powder. Mix the powder together using a dry paintbrush, and then dust it onto your unbaked clay charm. Bounce the bristles lightly against the clay's surface to get the lovely soft coloring shown.

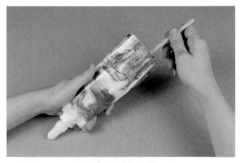

2. Mix the paint. Mix the paint using a chopstick or similar tool. Be sure to mix into all the corners so the color is evenly distributed. Once the mixture looks even inside, put a rubber band or clip on the top of the bag to keep any from spilling out while you pipe. Keep in mind that the first little bit stuck in the piping tip will still be white.

Applying Rhinestones and Charms with Glue

For a simple look, you can apply rhinestones and charms to your project with glue alone. It takes a bit of skill, but once you get used to working with the product, you'll be deco-ing everything in sight! Refer back here if any of the rhinestone projects later in the book has you confused.

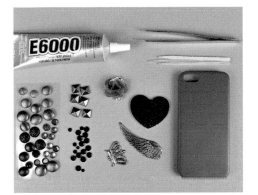

1. Gather your supplies. You'll want to have all your supplies in front of you before you begin, as you don't want to be running around the house getting trinkets while your glue slowly dries. Each project will list the supplies you need, but it never hurts to have more than you think you'll need on hand.

2. Trace your design. Get an idea of where you want your biggest charms, and then trace around them to mark the location of each one. Depending on the surface you're applying to, you'll want to use a pencil, washable marker, or even chalk. Anything that wipes away easily is ideal.

3. Place the big pieces. Spread a thin layer of glue on the areas you've marked for your biggest charms. Press them in place and continue working when they're set (usually about 10–30 minutes after placement, depending on your glue).

4. Fill the next section with glue. Work the rest of your project in small sections surrounding the larger charms for ease while working with the glue. Consider where you might place some of your medium-sized charms, then spread glue across the area.

5. Cover the section. Place your medium-sized charms in the glue-covered area and fill the smaller spaces between them with rhinestones of various sizes. Continue in this manner with the rest of the sections of your project until it's completely covered.

Creating Decoden with Collage Clay/Silicone

The process of creating a decoden composition with collage clay or silicone is incredibly easy once you get the right setup. You'll find this same process repeated in other projects, so you can refer back here if you ever need more guidance.

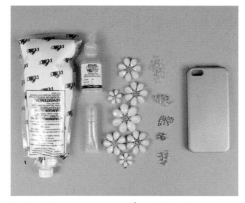

1. Gather your supplies. Get all your supplies before you begin; you don't want to be missing something while the clay is drying. The project will list the supplies you need, but it never hurts to have more than you think you'll need. It also helps to plan out where you want your biggest charms before you begin.

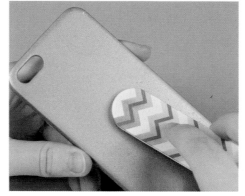

2. Scuff your project area. Using a nail file or medium-grit sandpaper, scuff the area where you plan to adhere the collage clay. This will create more surface area on your project and give the clay a better gripping ability.

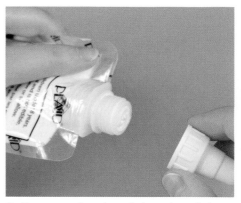

3. Prepare the clay. Select the piping tip you plan to use for your clay and secure it onto the bag. You may want to test out piping the clay onto some newspaper to get the hang of it. Try out some of the patterns shown following.

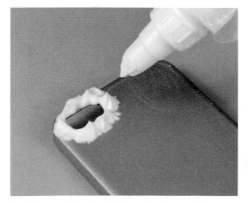

4. Cover the important areas. If you have vital areas of your project, such as the camera hole of a cell phone case, cover those first so you can focus on the rest of the project without worrying.

5. Fill the remaining surface. Fill in the remaining areas of your project with the piping method of your choosing. Make sure the project is completely covered where you plan to place your charms.

6. Add the big charms. Tuck your biggest charms into the clay using a placement you like. You can rest them flat, or place them at an angle so they face you for more height and volume. Try to get it right the first time—if you do make a mistake, you can rinse off your charm and try again, but your collage clay won't look as pretty.

Piping Methods

If you've ever tried piping frosting on a cake before, you'll find it's no different working with collage clay! Before you begin, get used to holding the bag with a firm but steady grip so you get an even piping of clay. Basically any piping technique for frosting can be applied to collage clay, but here are a few simple methods to get you started.

7. Fill in the gaps. Fill in the spaces between the big charms with medium-sized and small charms. Finally, add beads, pearls, and rhinestones in the small gaps between charms to fill in all the spaces.

Stars. With the star tip attached, hold the bag perpendicular to your surface. Squeeze a dollop of clay (the longer you squeeze, the bigger the star), dip the bag down ever so slightly, and then pull it back up to create a little point in the center of the star.

Waves. To create a long line of piped clay, hold the bag at about a 45 degree angle. Squeeze the bag while moving the tip slightly up and back, then down and forward, moving along the line. Continue in this manner, creating a sort of 2 steps forward, 1 step back motion.

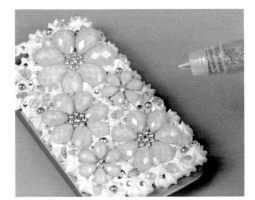

8. Finish the surface. Sprinkle glitter or small seed beads over your project while the collage clay is wet. When it's dry to the touch, in about an hour, you can add drizzles of puffy paint. The whole project needs about 48 hours to cure completely.

Rosettes. To create a large swirl for added height, hold the bag perpendicular to your surface. Start from the outside and make a spiral working your way inward. Finish by lifting the bag as you would for a star to create a point. You can keep building more and more rosettes onto your original one to create more height.

Rainbow Cell Phone Case

Here's the project that started it all! Take a crack at making your very own unique decoden piece by grabbing a simple hard shell case that fits your cell phone. Dressed up with some rhinestones or collage clay, every text you make will bring a little more brightness to your day!

Materials and Tools

✦ Plastic cell phone case

✦ Vanilla collage clay

✦ Approximately 28 cabochons, 4 each in pink, red, orange, yellow, green, blue, and violet

✦ Assorted beads, rhinestones, and pearls in white, silver, and rainbow colors (about 30–40 pieces)

16

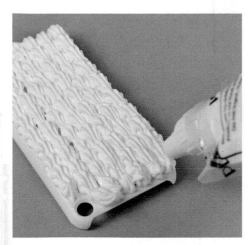

1 Apply the collage clay. Scuff the surface of your cell phone case and cover it with dollops of collage clay. A wave piping pattern was used here.

2 Add the cabochons. Starting at the top, press the pink charms into the clay, going across the width of the case. Next add the red charms, staggering the placement for a random look. Continue with the rainbow pattern down the entire case to the purple charms at the bottom.

3 Finish with the small pieces. In all the gaps between the charms, tuck in matching rhinestones, beads, and pearls to make the look very full.

Try Them All!

Test out the techniques in the Getting Started section to create all the options here! From chic to sweet, we've got you—and your cell phone—covered!

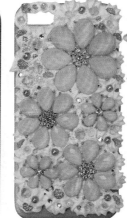

Classic Ombré: A collection of green, aqua, and blue charms were set together with charcoal pearls for this colorful style.

Royal Purple: This edgy case was made with large metal charms, pyramid studs, and purple and black rhinestones and pearls.

Gold and Green: A repurposed discount necklace provided the big, beautiful flower charms for this case.

Double-Decker Pink: Some charms were tucked into collage clay; more charms and rhinestones were added in the gaps or right on top.

Fiery Style: A simple phoenix outline was filled with rhinestones for this bright look that really pops!

Industrial Chic: Mod Melts from the Industrial mold were used with this case, with brown dry-brushing for a dingy look.

Breakfast Special Jar

Have a craving for waffles? You'll be happy to know the special of the day is a heaping stack of buttery waffles topped with fruit, whipped cream, and a drizzle of chocolate sauce. It looks so good you'll want to rush to your favorite diner by the time you're done!

Materials and Tools

✦ Glass jar with flat lid
✦ Golden brown, red, and navy polymer clay
✦ Vanilla collage clay
✦ Brown drizzle paint

Assembly

1 **Create the waffles.** To make the waffles, cut and bake a stick of clay that's about ¼" x ¼" (0.5 x 0.5cm) and about 2" (5cm) long. This will serve as a stamp for the waffle nooks. Roll out a sheet of ¼" (0.5cm) thick golden brown clay and cut 1" x 1" (2.5 x 2.5cm) squares for the waffles. Stamp 9 little divots into the squares to create each waffle. Create about 6 waffles.

2 **Create the strawberries.** The strawberries are simply teardrop shapes of red clay of different sizes with a flat top. Create the seeds by dimpling the clay with a toothpick at spaced-out intervals. Create about 9 strawberries sized about ⅜"–1" (1–2.5cm) or so.

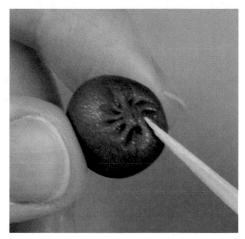

3 **Create the blueberries.** The blueberries are spheres of different sizes with toothpick dimples on the top in a starburst pattern. Create about 5 blueberries of different sizes. Bake all of your clay charms at this time.

4 **Apply the collage clay.** Apply collage clay over the top of the jar and spread it to create a flat layer. Once that is done, pipe stars around the perimeter of the top of the jar.

5 **Apply the charms.** Create the stack of waffles on the top of the jar by adding one in the middle, and then stacking more on top of it with a small dollop of collage clay between each waffle. Add a strawberry on top. Place the rest of the strawberries and blueberries on the sides.

6 **Drizzle the chocolate sauce.** Once the jar is dry, use the brown drizzle paint to drizzle chocolate sauce over the waffles, letting it drip down the sides of the jar.

Chocoholic Trinket Box

If you're addicted to chocolate like me, then this is just the project for you. You'll learn how to make a huge chocolate bar that will cover the top of your box, with all your favorite chocolate-themed charms added on top.

Materials and Tools

+ Square trinket box (painted brown)

+ Vanilla collage clay (mine has been tinted brown, see page 12)

+ Brown polymer clay

+ Craft glue

+ Popsicle stick or other similar tool

+ Assorted red, brown, and chocolate-themed cabochons (about 10 or more depending on the size of your box)

+ Assorted beads, rhinestones, and pearls in red, gold, and brown (about 20–30 pieces)

20

1 **Roll out the chocolate clay.** Roll out the brown clay until it's about ¼" (0.5cm) thick and large enough to cover the lid of your trinket box. Cut the clay so it's the size and shape of your box lid, minus ¼" (0.5cm) in height and width.

2 **Make the chocolate ridges.** Using the wooden craft stick, make ridges going across the width and height of the clay. Space them about 1" (2.5cm) apart, plus or minus ¼" (0.5cm) or so, to create an even number of ridges across the length and width of the sheet. Bake the sheet as directed or by using the Foolproof Baking technique, page 9.

3 **Apply the chocolate bar.** Once fully baked and cooled, prepare to apply the chocolate bar to the lid. Pipe some collage clay over the top of the lid, and then spread it smooth with a wooden craft stick or similar tool. Pipe a border of stars around the perimeter of the lid. Squish the chocolate bar in place, making sure the bar is centered.

4 **Add the cabochons.** Apply more collage clay to each corner of the chocolate bar, and then adhere your collection of cabochons to the clay. Add the beads, pearls, and rhinestones to finish.

No Time Like the Present Frame

They say to treat the time we have now as a gift—that's why it's called the present! This adorably themed frame would make a beautiful gift showing how much you treasure a certain memory.

Materials and Tools

✦ Frame with large border

✦ Vanilla collage clay

✦ Rhinestone glue

✦ About ½ yd. (50cm) of ribbon

✦ Lavender polymer clay

✦ Aqua and lavender cabochons (about 5)

✦ Assorted pearls in purple and silver (about 60 pieces)

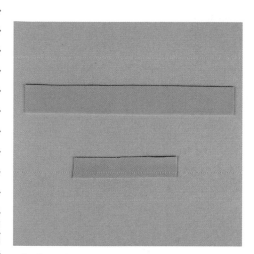

1 **Cut the bow shapes.** Roll a sheet from the purple clay that's about ⅛" (0.3cm) thick. From it, cut two rectangles: one that is as wide as the bow you want and twice as long as you want your bow to be, and one that is about half as long as the bow piece and a little less wide.

2 **Fold the bow shape.** Fold both ends of the bow rectangle toward the middle to create the bow shape. Press the edges in place.

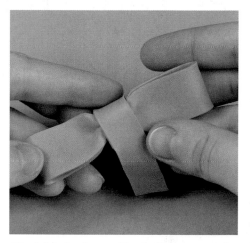

3 **Add the knot.** Pinch the center of the bow slightly and wrap the knot rectangle around it. Trim off the excess clay and seal the edges. Use the excess clay to create the end tails of the bow if desired.

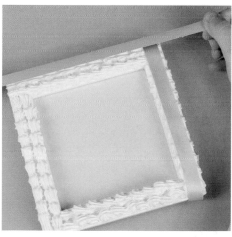

4 **Apply the ribbon.** Pipe collage clay onto your frame to cover the whole border area. Apply one piece of ribbon going across the top of the frame. Repeat with another piece of ribbon along the side, crossing them in the corner. Allow the ribbon ends to hang free for the time being.

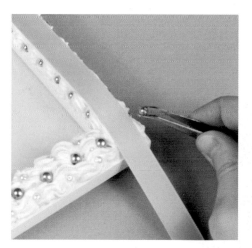

5 **Apply the cabochons.** Use dabs of collage clay to add the bow in the corner where the ribbons cross. Apply the rest of the cabochons and pearls to the other corner and on either side of the ribbon.

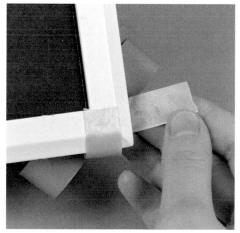

6 **Glue the excess ribbon.** Once the collage clay dries, fold the ribbon ends to the back of the frame and glue them in place.

Silver Sparkle Jewelry Set

This jewelry set includes a bangle bracelet and two rings in a beautiful teal and silver color scheme, plus a bonus necklace to match. The fluffy collage clay is fun enough for daytime, while the glitzy sparkles could easily pair with a night ensemble.

Materials and Tools

- ✦ Necklace with large pendant
- ✦ Bangle bracelet
- ✦ 2 ring blanks
- ✦ Vanilla collage clay
- ✦ Assorted small teal and silver cabochons of gems, hearts, flowers, and fleur-de-lys (about 15 pieces)
- ✦ Assorted beads, rhinestones, and pearls in silver, aqua, and teal (about 30 pieces)

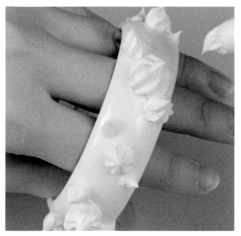

1 **Pipe clay on the bangle.** To decorate the bangle, pipe 8 large stars around the circumference of the bracelet, and then add small stars in the upper left and lower right corners of each large star to create a striped effect.

2 **Add the cabochons.** Add small cabochons in the center of each large star and rhinestones and pearls in the center of each small star to complete the look.

3 **Apply a large charm.** For a ring with one large charm, just a small dollop of collage clay will do. Lightly rest the charm in place and glue on a rhinestone for a final touch.

4 **Collage a ring.** For a collaged ring, apply a larger dollop of collage clay with one small cabochon in the middle. Apply pearls and rhinestones around it.

Make the Matching Necklace

The technique used for the collaged ring is the same for the necklace. A few dollops of collage clay on the pendant create the base, while small cabochons and rhinestones complete the look!

Deco Nails

Acrylic nails are classic decoden fodder. You'll see that resources and designs for nail art are practically limitless and can get hugely elaborate! If you're not quite ready to invest in loads of tiny brushes and gems, here is a simple crash course to get you started with a few easy but adorable styles.

- ✦ Nail polish of your choice
- ✦ Acrylic nails
- ✦ Mounting adhesive (also called sticky tack)
- ✦ Collage clay
- ✦ Small cabochons (about 6)
- ✦ Assorted small beads/rhinestones (about 40)

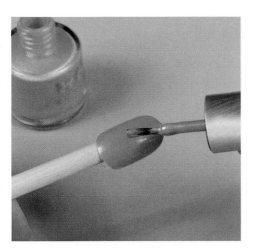

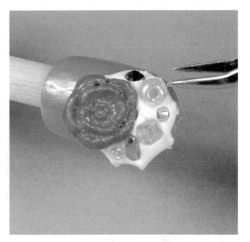

1 **Add your base coat.** While working on your nails, you'll want to stick them someplace sturdy. Try putting them on the end of a wooden dowel with some sticky tack. From there, cover your nails in 2–3 coats of nail polish until the color is nice and opaque. Continue when the paint is fully dry.

2 **Dot the collage clay.** Pipe a small dot of collage clay on the tip end of the nail.

3 **Add the cabochons.** For the larger nails, you can probably fit some small cabochons and a few rhinestones. For the smaller nails, just a couple of beads and rhinestones will do the trick.

New Nail Options

If they're tiny enough, you can use all kinds of deco supplies for nails! Let your nail polish collection inspire you to create some of these options.

Purple Chic: These deep purple nails were adorned with purple and silver studs in each corner, and then surrounded with black and lavender rhinestones.

Sleek Pink: Simple magenta nails were decorated with stripes of magenta and black rhinestones for a bold statement.

Gold Glam: Gold chrome nail polish was covered with some glittery gold drizzle paint and topped with bits of gold chain, bead cap findings, and gold pearls.

Upcycled Headband

Have an old necklace or bit of jewelry you never wear anymore? Decoden is the perfect way to revive those old castoffs! This headband is made from a disassembled necklace, and then livened up with collage clay and rhinestones.

Materials and Tools

✦ Flat plastic headband

✦ Vanilla collage clay

✦ Charm necklace or cabochons in small, medium, and large (about 7 pieces)

✦ Rhinestones and pearls in silver and white (about 30 pieces)

✦ Jewelry pliers

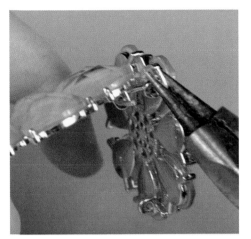

1 Disassemble the jewelry. If you're using old jewelry, you want to disassemble the pieces first. Look for small jump rings that hold together major pieces. These can easily be taken apart with jewelry pliers.

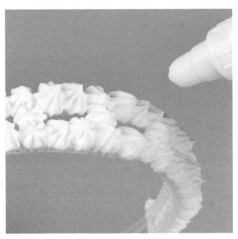

2 Apply the collage clay. Pipe the collage clay over the surface of the headband.

3 Add the cabochons. Set the cabochons (or jewelry pieces) into the clay. Here, the largest piece is set in the middle while the smaller pieces surround it, decreasing in size toward the ends.

4 Add the rhinestones. Tuck rhinestones into the gaps between the cabochons. Be sure to hang the headband on a surface that will hold it upright while it dries.

Try It with Barrettes!

Hair clips also deco beautifully! Easily make a simple look stellar with just a bit of sparkle in your hair!

Simple Celadon: A matching pair of celadon flowers add just a touch of glitz.

Silver Wings: A few metal wing findings on each barrette create an adorable look. Pyramid studs fill in the rest.

Caffeinated Tablet Case

I love a good cup of coffee now and then, and at my local coffee shop, I know I will never fail to see people typing away on their laptops or tablets while they enjoy their morning brew. Tablets and coffee seem to be linked somewhere in my brain, which is why I thought I should celebrate one of my favorite drinks with this project!

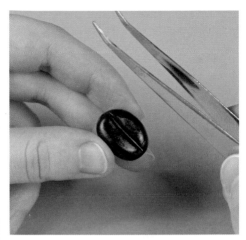

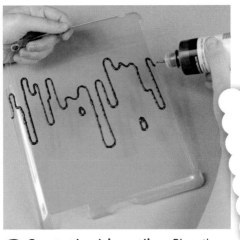

1 **Make the coffee beans.** Make a ¾" (2cm) sphere from brown polymer clay. Roll it slightly to make an oval, flatten one side, and then press a skewer or similar tool (like the flat side of tweezers) down the middle to make a ridge. Make and bake about 8 coffee beans before continuing.

2 **Create the drip outline.** Pipe the drizzle paint along the width of the tablet case, creating a dripping coffee look.

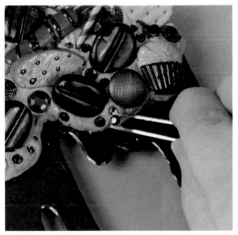

3 **Fill the outlines.** Once you're happy with the outlines you've created, fill them in with more drizzle paint. Allow the paint to fully dry before continuing.

4 **Add the cabochons.** Pipe the collage clay on the top of your case, overlapping the dripping coffee. Tuck your cabochons, pearls, and rhinestones into the clay.

Magnet Menagerie

Use the same technique as the ring on page 25 to make handy magnets to match any project! Each starts with a large star of collage clay with just one or two cabochons and a few rhinestones and pearls to complete them.

Bonjour Toiletries Set

Treat yourself to a lovely toiletries set decorated in the French style! This set includes a compact, soap dish, travel bottles, and toothbrush carrier that are perfect for decoden. With a lovely color scheme and a few choice cabochons, you're ready for Paris!

Materials and Tools

+ Vanity set: compact, soap dish, toothbrush carrier, travel bottles

+ Vanilla collage clay

+ Cabochons in pink, black, and French themes (about 40)

+ Rhinestones, pearls, and beads in pink, white, and black (about 60)

+ Pink drizzle paint

+ Rhinestone adhesive

Soap Dish

Toothbrush Holder

1 **Apply the collage clay.** For the soap dish, toothbrush holder, and compact, the collage clay is piped in a spiral pattern using lots of stars. This allows you to easily and evenly cover an unusual shape such as this oval.

2 **Add the cabochons.** Tuck the cabochons into the clay. For an added touch, dot black pearl beads around the perimeter of the clay.

3 **Add the drizzle paint.** Once the collage clay has dried, add swirls of pink paint within the collage clay ridges and over some charms for an added bit of color.

4 **Add decorative beads.** Using rhinestone adhesive, decorate some of the charms with extra beads for a final sparkle.

Curiouser & Curiouser Trinket Box

With so much of decoden being inspired by cute and sweet motifs, it was hard not to be inspired by one of my favorite books, *Alice in Wonderland*. With all the different charms to choose from—card suits, rabbits, and roses, among others—there's so much to work with to create an adorable masterpiece!

Materials and Tools

- ✦ Trinket box
- ✦ Light blue and white paint
- ✦ Painter's tape
- ✦ Paintbrush
- ✦ Blue lace to fit around box

- ✦ Cabochons in blue, red, and light blue in teacup, mushroom, card, rose, rabbit, crown, and cookie themes (about 15)
- ✦ Rhinestones and pearls in light blue and white (about 20)
- ✦ Rhinestone glue

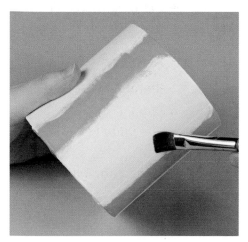

1 Paint the box. Paint the trinket box light blue and let it dry. Apply strips of painter's tape to the box to create vertical stripes. Paint between the tape stripes with the white paint, and then remove the tape.

2 Apply the lace. Using the rhinestone glue, apply lace around the top edge of the box. Fold under the end of the lace and glue it in place.

3 Apply the collage clay. Pipe the collage clay in zigzags around the circumference of the lid. To finish, pipe a large rosette in the middle for added height. Add card suit charms to the front of the rosette as the highlight.

4 Add the remaining cabochons. Apply the rest of the cabochons in the middle rosette and the pearls around the perimeter. Sprinkle in any remaining rhinestones for some added sparkle.

Secret Heart Sneakers

On their own, these sneakers look like they have a simple swirl pattern. Nothing special, right? But put them together and the two swirls make an adorable heart! You can surprise people every time you click your heels.

Materials and Tools

- ✦ Sneakers
- ✦ Flat-back rhinestones in blue, teal, light blue, and white in varying sizes (about 500)
- ✦ Rhinestone glue
- ✦ Assorted teal and silver beads and cabochons for charm (about 5)
- ✦ Head pin
- ✦ Jewelry pliers
- ✦ Large jump ring

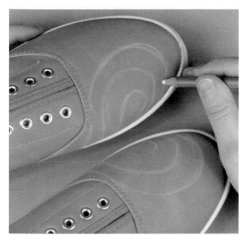

1 **Draw the outlines.** Using a pencil, marker, or anything else that won't leave a strong mark, draw the half-heart outline on the inside edge of one shoe. Repeat with the other shoe and put them together to make sure they create a heart shape. Draw smaller heart outlines inside the large heart the same way; this version has three sections, one for each shade of blue.

2 **Fill the center area.** With your darkest rhinestones, fill the center heart area.

3 **Outline the center.** Using white rhinestones, outline the center area. Move onto the teal rhinestones, adding another band. Keep moving outward in bands, alternating lighter shades of blue and white, until you reach the outer edge. Sprinkle the smallest rhinestones across the top of the shoe to taper off the shape.

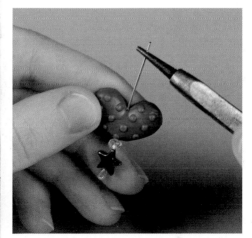

4 **Create a charm.** For an added touch, create a charm out of teal and silver cabochons and few beads. Thread them onto your head pin and bend over the end to lock them in place.

5 **Attach the charm.** Thread the large jump ring through the charm and use it to attach the charm to one of the lacing holes of the shoes.

Galaxy Notebook

The idea for this notebook came together when I noticed some of the cabochons I collected could look like planets. With a smattering of rhinestone stars, it all came together to create this project! Using metallic paints for a cloudy, ethereal background, you can create a galaxy of your own.

Materials and Tools

- ✦ Notebook (painted black)
- ✦ Black, purple, pink, white, and blue paint
- ✦ Small cabochons in purple, pink, and blue
- ✦ Foam brushes, sponges, and paintbrushes for painting
- ✦ Flat-back rhinestones in pink, white, and purple
- ✦ Rhinestone glue

38

1 **Paint the background swirls.** With the foam brush, create a few nebulae across the journal cover with the pink, blue, and purple paint. Sponge more black on top to mix the paints and get an even, gradated look.

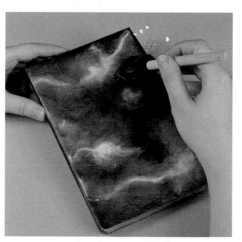

2 **Paint the highlights.** Tint the pink, purple, and blue paints with the white and paint some streaks going through the nebulae for some highlights. With a clean, damp sponge, soften the edges of the highlights. Continue to add more black and colored paint until you have a composition you like.

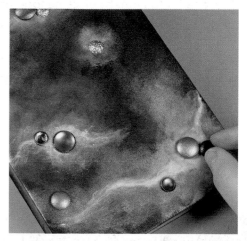

3 **Add the cabochons.** Glue cabochons in the middle of the nebulae as planets.

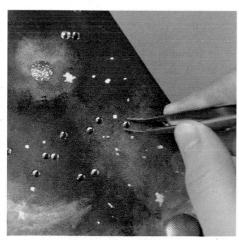

4 **Add the rhinestones.** Add rhinestones around the cabochons and interspersed over the galaxy for the stars. Add a few softer stars in white paint for the final touch.

Purple Swirls Variation

This journal was made by piping stripes of white and purple collage clay, and then using a toothpick to swirl the colors together. It was finished off with loads of purple and aqua cabochons and findings.

Union Jack Clutch

This clutch is totally mod with a touch of glam. The random mix of rhinestones and cabochons gives it a wonderful eclectic feel that's sure to be a favorite with hipsters and fashionistas alike.

Materials and Tools

- ✦ Clutch wallet
- ✦ Red and blue permanent markers
- ✦ Ruler
- ✦ Flat-back cabochons and rhinestones of various sizes in red (about 200 pieces)
- ✦ Flat-back cabochons and rhinestones of various sizes in blue (about 250 pieces)
- ✦ Flat-back cabochons and rhinestones of various sizes in white (about 300 pieces)
- ✦ Rhinestone glue

1 **Draw the Union Jack.** On one side of your clutch, use a ruler to draw the Union Jack outlines. Color in the outlines with the corresponding red and blue permanent markers.

2 **Fill in the red sections.** Use a combination of the red cabochons and rhinestones to fill the red sections all the way to the edges.

3 **Fill in the white sections.** Repeat this with the white sections and white rhinestones and cabochons. You'll need to use lots of smaller pieces.

4 **Fill in the blue sections.** Lastly, fill in the remaining sections with blue cabochons and rhinestones.

More Rhinestone Ideas

One of the leftover strawberries from the Breakfast Special Jar (page 18) gets the glam treatment here. Add a pin to the back, green rhinestones on top, and red rhinestones to fill in the rest.

Fashionista Set: Cloche Hat and Sunglasses

This pair of simple black sunglasses with a matching hat is a classic stylish duo. Set yours apart from the rest with a few rhinestones done in an ombré style using pink and purple.

Materials and Tools

✦ Sunglasses

✦ Hat with ribbon accent

✦ Flat-back rhinestones in purple, magenta, pink, black, and white (about 300)

✦ Cabochons in pink, purple, and magenta (about 5)

✦ Rhinestone glue

Assembly

1 **Apply the sunglasses charms.** In the upper corner of the sunglasses, apply a few showpiece charms. Make sure they dry fully before continuing.

2 **Surround the charms.** Surround the charms with rhinestones, going across the top and down the sides of the eyepieces.

3 **Cover the sides.** Apply rhinestones to the sides of the sunglasses, tapering off from pink down to white rhinestones.

4 **Apply the cabochons.** Apply cabochons to the hat at the side, overlapping the ribbon accent. Apply black rhinestones in between the charms.

5 **Cover the hat ribbon.** Working from the cabochons outward, apply the magenta, violet, and purple rhinestones down each side of the hat along the ribbon. Gradate the colors using all the sizes that you have for a smooth transition.

Digital Duo: Flash Drive and Earbuds

If you've got a flash drive you use frequently for school, dress it up and make it your own with a few rhinestones and studs. Not only will you never get yours confused with anyone else's, it'll make schoolwork so much more bearable! Make it a matching set by decorating a pair of earbuds as well.

Materials and Tools

✦ Flash drive with cap

✦ Earbuds

✦ Square pyramid studs (about 10)

✦ Flat-back rhinestones of various sizes and colors (about 100)

✦ Rhinestone glue

44

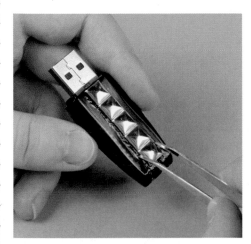

1 Attach the studs. Adhere studs going down the center of the flash drive on both sides.

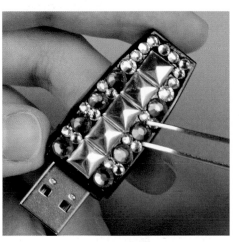

2 Add the rhinestones. Add rhinestones on each side of the studs, covering both sides of the flash drive. Here, they were done in a striped pattern.

3 Decorate the cap. Finish the look by adding more rhinestones to the flash drive cap.

4 Decorate the earbuds. Try on your earbuds first to find an area you can decorate without scratching your ears. Apply rhinestones to one section at a time as you try them on to make sure they're comfortable as well as stylish!

Simple and Sophisticated

This cell phone wallet was adorned with a classy white rhinestone butterfly pendant, and then surrounded with more white rhinestones of various sizes all around. The rhinestones taper off gracefully toward the edges.

Statement Belts

These bright-colored belts add a wonderful bit of pop to an outfit, and the rhinestone sparkle gives them a touch of glam. Go with simple and sophisticated stripes or edgy leopard spots—whatever suits your mood, because they're both easy to make!

Materials and Tools

✦ Belt

✦ **Stripes**: flat-back rhinestones in two colors, same size (about 200 each)

✦ **Spots**: flat-back rhinestones in two colors, varying sizes (about 50 of first color, 150 of second)

✦ Rhinestone glue

Stripes

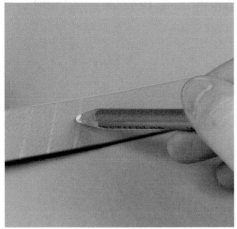

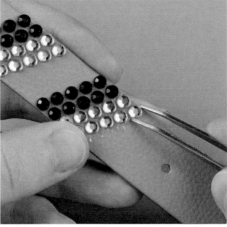

1 **Draw the outlines.** Using a pencil, marker, or anything else that won't leave a strong mark, draw diagonal lines across the width of your belt, all the way along the length until you reach the holes.

2 **Fill the outlines.** Fill the first section with your first color of rhinestones, then the second section with your second color. Leave the third section blank. Continue with this pattern until you reach the holes of your belt.

Spots

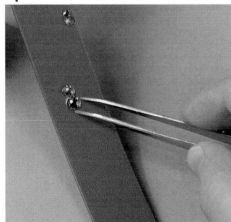

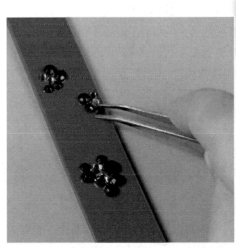

1 **Create the inner spots.** Using different sized stones, make small, irregular shapes with just 2–3 stones in your first color. Place these randomly over your belt, stopping when you get to the holes.

2 **Add the outer markings.** Using your second color, outline the shapes, but leave a few gaps here and there to create a natural, organic looking spot. Repeat this with all of the shapes over the belt.

Supplies

Here is a list of a variety of particular brands of supplies used to make the projects in this book. You can use these products or your own preferred brands. These products can typically be found at your local craft or hobby store, art supply store, or online.

- ❏ Collage clay/decoden "whippy": Mod Podge® Collage Clay by Plaid
- ❏ Faux resin: Mod Podge® Mod Melts by Plaid
- ❏ Faux resin molds: Mod Podge® Mod Molds by Plaid
- ❏ Glitter: Mod Podge® Podgeable Glitters by Plaid

- ❏ Glue: E-6000®; G-S Hypo Cement; Quik-Cure 5 Min. Epoxy by Hobbylinc
- ❏ Paint: Mod Podge® Drizzle Paint by Plaid
- ❏ Polymer clays: Fimo; Sculpey

More Great Books from Design Originals

Awesome Duct Tape Projects
ISBN 978-1-57421-895-4 **$9.99**
DO5453

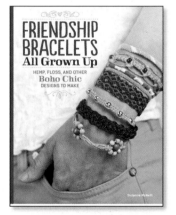

Friendship Bracelets
ISBN 978-1-57421-866-4 **$9.99**
DO5440

Rubber Band Jewelry All Grown Up
ISBN 978-1-57421-916-6 **$9.99**
DO5474

Sew Kawaii!
ISBN 978-1-56523-568-7 **$19.95**

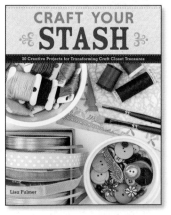

Craft Your Stash
ISBN 978-1-57421-873-2 **$19.99**
DO5447

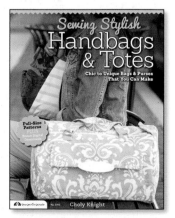

Sewing Stylish Handbags & Totes
ISBN 978-1-57421-422-2 **$22.99**
DO5393

Acquisition editor: **Peg Couch** • Copy editor: **Katie Weeber** • Cover and layout designer: **Ashley Millhouse**
Cover and project photography: **Scott Kriner** • Step-by-step photography: **Matthew McClure** • Editor: **Colleen Dorsey**

ISBN 978-1-57421-948-7

© 2014 by Choly Knight and New Design Originals Corporation, *www.d-originals.com*, an imprint of Fox Chapel Publishing, 800-457-9112, 1970 Broad Street, East Petersburg, PA 17520.

Printed in the United States of America
First printing

Bling Out Your World

Make your accessories super *kawaii* with the Japanese art of decoden! Inside you'll find 16 outrageously whimsical projects for embellishing your phone case, acrylic nails, sunglasses, toiletries kit, and even your sneakers with impractical indulgence. Whether you're looking for simple rhinestone flair or excessive frosted goodness, you'll find plenty of inspiration in this book to get your creative juices flowing.

dec•o•den
noun

A highly stylized, colorful, and over-the-top Japanese decorative craft that literally means "phone decoration," but which has grown to encompass all sorts of fun projects. It involves decorating objects with tons of charms and bling.

✦ 16 step-by-step projects for blingy fashion accessories

✦ Fabulous decoden compositions with charms, trinkets, baubles, and findings

✦ Inspired ideas for phone cases, acrylic nails, toiletries sets, sunglasses, sneakers, and more

✦ Practical tips on materials, supplies, and techniques

✦ How to make your own charms with Mod Melts and polymer clay

No. 5483

Design Originals
an Imprint of Fox Chapel Publishing
www.d-originals.com

ISBN: 978-1-57421-948-7